PSALMS

FOR THE

STRESSED

AND

AFFLICTED

Author: GOD

Psalms inspired by the Holy Spirit

Compilation of Psalms by mgc 2016

Printed in the United States of America

Available at Amazon and other retail stores

Reference: The Holy Bible
The Immaculate Conception Edition
C. D. Stampley Enterprises, Inc.
Charlotte, North Carolina
1965
"Psalms are public domain" quote from
C. D. Stampley Enterprises
English translation from the Latin
conversion

A portion of the proceedings will go toward free books to hospitals where prayers are desperately needed.

To my LORD and Savior in thanksgiving for his wondrous deeds who is with me always as he will be with you in your time of need.

.

Psalms for the Stressed and Afflicted

Psalm 89:1-2

O LORD, you have been our refuge through all generations. Before the mountains were begotten and the earth and the world were brought forth, from everlasting to everlasting you are God.

Psalm 50(51):15
I will teach transgressors your ways, and sinners shall return to you.

This book was written to serve as a companion in times of supplication and requests to the Lord.

It is my aspiration these compilations of David's psalms will guide you in perfect prayer and help you as they helped me during my time of stress and affliction.

This book consists of four sections:

Psalms for the Stressed and the Afflicted
Psalms, Words of Comfort
Psalms, Words of Praise and Wisdom
Psalms, Words of Warning

Psalms for the Stressed and Afflicted

Psalm 4:1
When I call, answer me, O my just God, you who relieve me when I am in distress; have pity on me, and hear my prayer!

Psalm 5:1-4
Hearken to my words, O LORD, attend to my sighing. Heed my call for help, my king and my God!
To you I pray, O LORD; at dawn you hear my voice; at dawn I bring my plea expectantly before you.

Psalm 6:1-11
O LORD, reprove me not in your anger, nor chastise me in your wrath. Have pity on me, O LORD, for I am languishing; heal me, O LORD, for my body is in terror; my soul, too, is utterly terrified; but you, O LORD, how long? Return, O LORD, save my life; rescue me because of your kindness, for among the dead no one remembers you; in the nether world who gives you thanks? I am wearied with sighing; every night I flood my bed with weeping; I drench my couch with my tears. My eyes are dimmed with sorrow; they have aged because of all my foes. Depart from me, all evildoers, for the LORD has heard the sound of my weeping. The LORD has heard my plea; the LORD has accepted my prayer. All my enemies shall be put to shame in utter terror; they shall fall back in sudden shame.

Psalms for the Stressed and Afflicted

Psalm 7:1-2
O LORD, my God, in you I take refuge; save me from all my pursuers and rescue me, lest I become like the Lion's prey, to be torn to pieces, with no one to rescue me.

Psalm 18 (19): 12-15
Though your servant is careful of them, very diligent in keeping them, yet who can detect failings? Cleanse me from my unknown faults! From wanton sin specially, restrain your servant; let it not rule over me. Then shall I be blameless and innocent of serious sin. Let the words of my mouth and the thought of my heart find favor before you, O LORD, my rock and my redeemer.

Psalm 21(22):12
Be not far from me, for I am in distress; be near, for I have no one to help me.

Psalm 24 (25):16-18, 21
Look toward me, and have pity on me, for I am alone and afflicted. Relieve the troubles of my heart, and bring me out of my distress. Put an end to my affliction and my suffering, and take away all my sins. Let integrity and uprightness preserve me, because I wait for you, O LORD.

Psalms for the Stressed and Afflicted

Psalm 26(27):7-9
Hear, O LORD, the sound of my call; have pity on me, and answer me. Of you my heart speaks; you my glance seeks; your presence, O LORD, I seek. Hide not your face from me; do not in anger repel your servant. You are my helper; cast me not off, forsake me not, O God my savior.

Psalm 29(30):11
Hear, O LORD, and have pity on me; O LORD, be my helper.

Psalm 30(31):1-3, 10-11,15,17
In you, O LORD, I take refuge; let me never be put to shame. In your justice rescue me, incline your ear to me, make haste to deliver me! Be my rock of refuge, a stronghold to give me safety. Have pity on me, O LORD, for I am in distress; with sorrow my eye is consumed; my soul also, and my body. For my life is spent with grief and my years with sighing; my strength has failed through affliction, and my bones are consumed. But my trust is in you, O LORD; I say, "You are my God." Let your face shine upon your servant; save me in your kindness.

Psalms for the Stressed and Afflicted

Psalm 31(32):3
As long as I would not speak, my bones wasted away with my groaning all the day, for day and night your hand was heavy upon me; my strength was dried up as by the heat of summer. Then I acknowledged my sin to you, my guilt I covered not. I said, "I confess my faults to the LORD," and you took away the guilt of my sin. For this shall every faithful man pray to you in time of stress. Though deep waters overflow, they shall not reach him. You are my shelter; from distress you will preserve me; with glad cries of freedom you will ring me round.

Psalm 37(38): 1-23
O LORD, in your anger punish me not, in your wrath chastise me not; for your arrows have sunk deep in me, and your hand has come down upon me. There is no health in my flesh because of your indignation; there is no wholeness in my bones because of my sin, for my iniquities have overwhelmed me; they are like a heavy burden, beyond my strength. Noisome and festering are my sores because of my folly, I am stooped and bowed down profoundly; all the day I go in mourning, for my loins are filled with burning pains; there is not health in my flesh. I am numbed and severely crushed; I roar with anguish of heart. O LORD, all my desire is before you; from you my groaning is not hid.

Psalms for the Stressed and Afflicted

My heart throbs; my strength forsakes me; the very light of my eyes has failed me. My friends and my companions stand back because of my affliction; my neighbors stand afar off. Men lay snares for me seeking my life; they look to my misfortune, they speak of ruin, treachery they talk of all the day. But I am like a deaf man, hearing not, like a dumb man who opens not his mouth. I am become like a man who neither hears nor has in his mouth a retort. Because for you, O LORD, I wait; you, O LORD my God, will answer when I say, "Let them not be glad on my account who, when my foot slips, glory over me". For I am very near to falling, and my grief is with me always.

Indeed, I acknowledge my guilt; I grieve over my sin, but my undeserved enemies are strong; many are my foes without cause. Those who repay evil for good harass me for pursuing good. Forsake me not, O LORD; my God, be not far from me! Make haste to help me, O Lord, my salvation!

Psalm 38(39):13-14
Hear my prayer, O LORD; to my cry give ear; to my weeping be not deaf! For I am but a wayfarer before you, a pilgrim like all my fathers. Turn your gaze from me, that I may find respite ere I depart and be no more.

Psalms for the Stressed and Afflicted

Psalm 39(40):12-18
Withhold not, O LORD, your compassion from me; may your kindness and your truth ever preserve me. For all about me are evils beyond reckoning; my sins so overcome me that I cannot see; they are more numerous than the hairs of my head, and my heart fails me. Deign, O LORD, to rescue me; O LORD, make haste to help me. Let all be put to shame and confusion who seek to snatch away my life. Let them be turned back in disgrace who desire my ruin. Let them be dismayed in their shame who say to me, "aha, aha" but may all who seek you exult and be glad in you, and may those who love your salvation say ever, "The LORD be glorified." Though I am afflicted and poor, yet the LORD thinks of me. You are my help and my deliverer; O my God, hold not back!

Psalm 41(42):6
Why are you so downcast, O my soul? Why do you sigh within me? Hope in God! For I shall again be thanking him, in the presence of my savior and my God.

Psalm 50(51):1-19
Have mercy on me, O God, in your goodness; in the greatness of your compassion wipe out my offense. Thoroughly wash me from my guilt and of my sin cleanse me.

Psalms for the Stressed and Afflicted

For I acknowledge my offense, and my sin is before me always; "against you only have I sinned, and done what is evil in your sight"—that you may be justified in your sentence vindicated when you condemn. Indeed, in guilt was I born, and in sin my mother conceived me; behold, you are pleased with sincerity of heart, and in my inmost being you teach me wisdom. Cleanse me of sin with hyssop, that I may be purified; wash me, and I shall be whiter than snow. Let me hear the sounds of joy and gladness; the bones you have crushed shall rejoice. Turn away your face from my sin, and blot out all my guilt. A clean heart create for me, O God, and a steadfast spirit renew within me. Cast me not out from your presence, and your Holy Spirit take not from me. Give me back the joy of your salvation, and a willing spirit sustain in me. I will teach transgressors your ways, and sinners shall return to you. Free me from blood guilt, O God, my saving God; then my tongue shall revel in your justice. O LORD, open my lips, and my mouth shall proclaim your praise. For you are not pleased with sacrifices; should I offer a holocaust, you would not accept it. My sacrifice, O God, is a contrite spirit; a heart contrite and humbled, O God, you will not spurn.

Psalms for the Stressed and Afflicted

Psalm 53(54):1-9
O God, by your name save me and by your might defend my cause. O God, hear my prayer; hearken to the words of my mouth. For haughty men have risen up against me, and fierce men seek my life; they set not God before their eyes. Behold, God is my helper; the LORD sustains my life. Turn back the evil upon my foes, in your faithfulness destroy them. Freely will I offer you sacrifice; I will praise your name, O LORD, for its goodness, because from all distress you have rescued me, and my eyes look down upon my enemies.

Psalm 54(55):1-3, 5-8
Hearken, O God, to my prayer; turn not away from my pleading; give heed to me, and answer me. My heart quakes within me; the terror of death has fallen upon me. Fear and trembling come upon me, and horror overwhelms me, and I say "Had I but wings like a dove, I would fly away and be at rest. Far away I would flee; I would lodge in the wilderness."

Psalm 55(56):5, 13-14
In God, in whose promise I glory, in God I trust without fear; what can flesh do against me? I am bound, O God, by vows to you; your thank offerings I will fulfill. For you have rescued me from death, my feet, too, from stumbling; that I may walk before God in the light of the living.

Psalms for the Stressed and Afflicted

Psalm 63(64):1-11
Hear O God, my voice in my lament; from the dread enemy preserve my life. Shelter me against the council of malefactors, against the tumult of evildoers, who sharpen their tongues like swords, who aim like arrows their bitter words, shooting from ambush at the innocent man, suddenly shooting at him without fear. They resolve on their wicked plan; they conspired to set snares, saying, "who will see us?" They devise a wicked scheme, and conceal the scheme they have devised; deep are the thoughts of each heart. But God shoots his arrows at them; suddenly they are struck. He brings them down by their own tongues; all who see them nod their heads. And all men fear and proclaim the work of God, and ponder what he has done. The just man is glad in the LORD and takes refuge in him; in him glory all the upright of heart.

Psalms for the Stressed and Afflicted

Psalm 68(69):1-4, 6, 14-18, 30-32
Save me, O God, for the waters threaten my life; I am sunk in the abysmal swamp where there is no foot hold; I have reached the watery depths; the flood overwhelms me. I am wearied with calling, my throat is parched; my eyes have failed with looking for my God. O God, you know my folly, and my faults are not hid from you. But I pray to you O God, for the time of your favor, O God! In your kindness answer me with your constant help. Rescue me out of the mire; may I not sink! May I be rescued from my foes, and from the watery depths. Let not the flood-waters overwhelm me, nor the abyss swallow me up, nor the pit close its mouth over me. Answer me, O LORD, for bounteous is your kindness; in your great mercy turn toward me. Hide not your face from your servant; in my distress, make haste to answer me.

Psalm 69(70):1-6
Deign, O God, to rescue me; O LORD, make haste to help me. Let them be put to shame and confounded who seek my life. Let them be turned back in disgrace who desire my ruin. Let them retire in their shame who say to me "Aha, Aha"! But may all who seek you exult and be glade in you, and may those who love your salvation say ever, "God be glorified". But I am afflicted and poor; O LORD, hasten to me! You are my help and my deliverer; O LORD, hold not back!

Psalms for the Stressed and Afflicted

Psalm 70(71):1-8, 12, 17-21
In you, O LORD, I take refuge; let me never be put to shame. In your justice, rescue me, and deliver me; incline your ear to me. Be my rock of refuge, a stronghold to give me safety, for you are my rock and my fortress. O my God, rescue me from the hand of the wicked, from the grasp of the criminal and the violent. For you are my hope, O LORD; my trust, O God, from my youth. On you I depend from birth; from my mother's womb you are my strength; constant has been my hope in you. A portent am I to many, but you are my strong refuge! My mouth shall be filled with your praise, with your glory day by day. O God, be not far from me; my God, make haste to help me. O God, you have taught me from my youth, and till the present I proclaim your wondrous deeds; and now that I am old and gray, O God, forsake me not till I proclaim your strength to every generation that is to come. Your power and your justice, O God, reach to heaven, you have done great things; O God, who is like you? Though you have made me feel many bitter afflictions, you will again revive me; from the depth of the earth you will once more raise me. Renew your benefits toward me, and comfort me over and over.

Psalms for the Stressed and Afflicted

Psalm 76(77):1-15
Aloud to God I cry; Aloud to God, to hear me; on the day of my distress I seek the LORD. By night my hands are stretched out without flagging; my soul refuses comfort. When I remember God, I moan; when I ponder, my spirit grows faint. You keep my eyes watchful; I am troubled and cannot speak. I consider the days of old; the years long past I remember. In the night I meditate in my heart; I ponder, and my spirit broods: "Will the LORD reject forever and nevermore be favorable? Will his kindness utterly cease, his promise fail for all generations? Has God forgotten pity? Does he in anger withhold his compassion?" And I say, "This is my sorrow, that the right hand of the Most High is changed." I remember the deeds of the LORD; yes, I remember your wonders of old. And I meditate on your works; your exploits I ponder. O God, your way is holy; what great god is there like our God? You are the God who works wonders; among the peoples you have made known your power.

Psalm 81(82):1-4
God arises in the divine assembly; he judges in the mist of the gods. "How long will you judge unjustly and favor the cause of the wicked? Defend the lowly and the fatherless; render justice to the afflicted and the destitute. Rescue the lowly and the poor; from the hand of the wicked deliver them."

Psalms for the Stressed and Afflicted

Psalm 85(86):1-17
Incline your ear, O LORD; answer me, for I am afflicted and poor. Keep my life, for I am devoted to you; save your servant who trust in you. You are my God; have pity on me. O LORD, for to you I call all the day. Gladden the soul of your servant, for to you, O LORD I lift up my soul; for you, O LORD, are good and forgiving, abounding in kindness to all who call upon you. Hearken, O LORD, to my prayer and attend to the sound of my pleading. In the day of my distress I call upon you, for you will answer me. There's none like you among the gods, O LORD and there are no works like yours. All the nations you have made shall come and worship you, O LORD, and glorify your name. For you are great and do wondrous deeds, you alone are God. Teach me, O LORD, your way that I may walk in your truth; direct my heart that it may fear your name. I will give thanks to you, O LORD my God, with all my heart, and I will glorify your name forever. Great has been your kindness toward me; you have rescued me from the depths of the nether world. O God, the haughty have risen up against me, and the company of fierce men seeks my life, nor do they set you before their eyes. But you O LORD, are a God merciful and gracious, slow to anger, abounding in kindness and fidelity. Turn toward me, and have pity on me; give your strength to your servant, and save the son of your handmaid. Grant me a proof of your favor, that my enemies may see, to their confusion, that you, O LORD, have helped and comforted me.

Psalms for the Stressed and Afflicted

Psalm 87(88):1-19
O LORD, my God, by day I cry out, at night I clamor in your presence. Let my prayer come before you; incline your ear to my call for help, for my soul is surfeited with troubles and my life draws near to the netherworld. I am numbered with those who go down into the pit; I am a man without strength. My couch is among the dead, like the slain who lie in the grave. Whom you remember no longer and who are cut off from your care. You have plunged me into the bottom of the pit, into the dark abyss. Upon me your wrath lies heavy, and with all your billows you overwhelm me. You have taken my friends away from me; you have made me an abomination to them; I am in prison, and I cannot escape. My eyes have grown dim through affliction; daily I call upon you, O LORD; to you I stretch out my hands, will you work wonders for the dead? Will the shades arise to give you thanks? Do they declare your kindness in the grave, your faithfulness among those who have perished? Are your wonders made known in the darkness, or your justice in the land of oblivion? But I, O LORD, cry out to you; with my morning prayer I wait upon you. Why, O LORD, do you reject me; why hide from me your face? I am afflicted and in agony from my youth; I am dazed with the burden of your dread. Your furies have swept over me, your terrors have cut me off; they encompass me like water all the day; on all sides they closed in upon me. Companion and neighbor you have taken away from me; my only friend is darkness.

Psalms for the Stressed and Afflicted

Psalm 89(90): 12-14, 17
Teach us to number our days aright, that we may gain wisdom of heart. Return, O LORD! How long? Have pity on your servants! Fill us at daybreak with your kindness, that we may shout for joy and gladness all our days. And may the gracious care of the Lord our God be ours; prosper the work of our hands for us! [Prosper the work of our hands!]

Psalm 90(91):1-16
You who dwell in the shelter of the most high, who abide in the shadow of the almighty, say to the LORD, "my refuge and my fortress, my God, in whom I trust." For he will rescue you from the snare of the fowler, from the destroying pestilence. With his pinions he will cover you, and under his wings you shall take refuge; his faithfulness is a buckler and a shield. You shall not fear the terror of the night nor the arrow that flies by day; not the pestilence that roams in darkness nor the devastating plague at noon. Though a thousand fall at your side, ten thousand at your right side, near you it shall not come. Rather with your eyes shall you behold and see the requital of the wicked, because you have the LORD for your refuge; you have made the most high your stronghold. No evil shall befall you, nor shall affliction come near your tent, for to his angels he has given command about you, that they guard you in all your ways. Upon their hands they shall bear you up, lest you dash

Psalms for the Stressed and Afflicted

your foot against a stone. You shall tread upon the asp and the viper; you shall trample down the lion and the dragon. Because he clings to me, I will deliver him; I will set him on high because he acknowledges my name. He shall call upon me, and I will answer him; I will be with him in distress; I will deliver him and Glorify him; with length of days I will gratify him and will show him my salvation.

Psalm 101(102):1-13, 24-29
O LORD, hear my prayer, and let my cry come to you. Hide not your face from me in the day of my distress. Incline your ear to me; in the day when I call, answer me speedily. For my days vanish like smoke, and my bones burn like fire. Withered and dried up like grass is my heart; I forget to eat my bread. Because of my insistent sighing I am reduced to skin and bone. I am like a desert owl; I have become like an owl among the ruins. I am sleepless, and I moan; I am like a sparrow alone on the housetop. All the day my enemies revile me; in their rage against me they make a curse of me. For I eat ashes like bread and mingle my drink with tears, because of your fury and your wrath; for you lifted me up only to cast me down. My days are like a lengthening shadow and I wither like grass. But you, O LORD, abide forever, and your name through all generations. He has broken down my strength in the way; he has cut short my days. I say: O my God, take me not hence in the midst of my days; through all generations your years endure. Of

Psalms for the Stressed and Afflicted

old you established the earth, and the heavens are the work of your hands. They shall perish, but you remain though all of them grow old like a garment. Like clothing you change them, and they are changed, but you are the same, and your years have no end. The children of your servants shall abide, and their posterity shall continue in your presence.

Psalm 118(119):84-88,121-122,133-134,145-160
How many are the days of your servant? When will you do judgment on my persecutors? The proud have dug pits for me; this is against your law. All your commands are steadfast; they persecute me wrongfully; help me! They have all but put an end to me on the earth, but I have not forsaken your percepts. In your kindness give me life, that I may keep the decrees of your mouth. I have fulfilled just ordinances; leave me not to my oppressors. Be surety for the welfare of your servant; let not the proud oppress me. Steady my footsteps according to your promise, and let no iniquity rule over me. Redeem me from the oppression of men, that I may keep your percepts. I call out with all my heart, answer me, O LORD; I will observe your statues. I call upon you; save me, and I will keep your decrees. Before dawn I come and cry out; I hope on your words. My eyes greet the night watches in meditation on your promise. Hear my voice according to your kindness, O LORD; according to your ordinance give me life. I am attacked by malicious persecutors who are far from your law. You, O LORD, are near, and all your commands are

Psalms for the Stressed and Afflicted

permanent. Of old I know from your decrees, that you have established them forever. Behold my affliction, and rescue me, for I have not forgotten your law. Plead my cause, and redeem me; for the sake of your promise give me life. Far from sinners is salvation because they seek not your statutes. Your compassion is great, O LORD; according to your ordinances give me life. Though my persecutors and my foes are many, I turn not away from your decrees. I behold the apostates with loathing, because they kept not to your promise. See how I love your percepts, O LORD; in your kindness give me life. Permanence is your word's chief trait; each of your just ordinances is everlasting.

Psalm 119(120):1-2
In my distress I called to the LORD and he answered me. O LORD, deliver me from lying lip, from treacherous tongue.

Psalms for the Stressed and Afflicted

Psalm 120(121):1-2,5-8
I lift up my eyes toward the mountains; whence shall help come to me? My help is from the Lord, who made heaven and earth. The Lord is your guardian; the Lord is your shade; he is beside you at your right hand. The sun shall not harm you by day, nor the moon by night. The Lord will guard you from all evil; he will guard your life. The Lord will guard your coming and your going, both now and forever.

Psalm 122(123):1-4
To you I lift up my eyes who are enthroned in heaven. Behold, as the eyes of servants are on the hands of their masters, as the eyes of a maid are on the hands of her mistress, so are our eyes on the Lord, our God, till he have pity on us. Have pity on us, O LORD, have pity on us, for we are more than sated with contempt, our souls are more than sated with mockery of the arrogant, with the contempt of the proud.

Psalm 129(130):1-6
Out of the depths I cry to you, O LORD; LORD, hear my voice! Let your ears be attentive to my voice in supplication: if you, O LORD, mark iniquities, LORD, who can stand? But with you is forgiveness, that you may be revered. I trust in the LORD; my soul trusts in his word. My soul waits for the LORD more than sentinels wait for the dawn.

Psalms for the Stressed and Afflicted

Psalm 139(140):1-14
Deliver me, O LORD, from evil men; preserve me from violent men, from those who devise evil in their hearts, and stir up war every day. They make their tongues sharp as those of serpents; the venom of asps is under their lips. Save me, O LORD, from the hands of the wicked; preserve me from violent men who plan to trip up my feet—the proud who have hidden a trap for me; they have spread cords for a net; by the wayside they have laid snares for me. I say to the LORD, you are my God; hearken, O LORD, to my voice in supplication. O God, my LORD, my strength and my salvation; you are my helmet in the day of battle! Grant not, O LORD, the desires of the wicked; further not their plans. Those who surround me lift up their heads; may the mischief which they threaten overwhelm them. May he rain burning coals upon them; may he cast them into the depths, never to rise. A man of wicked tongue shall not abide in the land; evil shall abruptly entrap the violent man. I know that the LORD renders justice to the afflicted, judgment to the poor. Surely the just shall give thanks to your name; the upright shall dwell in your presence.

Psalms for the Stressed and Afflicted

Psalm 140(141):1-10
O LORD, to you I call; hasten to me; hearken to my voice when I call upon you. Let my prayer come like incense before you; the lifting up of my hands like the evening sacrifice. O LORD, set a watch before my mouth, a guard at the door of my lips. Let not my heart incline to the evil of engaging in deeds of wickedness with men who are evildoers; and let me not partake of their dainties. Let the just man strike me; that is kindness; let him reprove me; it is oil for the head, which my head shall not refuse, but I will still pray under these afflictions. Their judges were cast down over the crag, and they heard how pleasant were my words. As when a plow man breaks furrows in the field, so their bones are strewn by the edge of the netherworld. For toward you, O God, my LORD, my eyes are turned; in you I take refuge; strip me not of life. Keep me from the trap they have set for me, and from the snares of the evildoers. Let all the wicked fall, each into his own net, while I escape.

Psalm 141(142):1-8
With a loud voice I cry out to the LORD; with a loud voice I beseech the LORD. My complaint I pour out before him, before him I lay bare my distress. When my spirit is faint within me, you know my path. In the way along which I walk they have hid a trap for me. I look to the right to see, but there is no one who pays me heed. I have lost all means of escape; there is no one who cares for my

Psalms for the Stressed and Afflicted

life. I cry out to you, O LORD, I say "You are my refuge, my portion in the land of the living". Attend to my cry, for I am brought low indeed. Rescue me from persecutors, for they are too strong for me: lead me forth from prison, that I may give thanks to your name. The just shall gather around me when you have been good to me.

Psalm 142(143):1-12
O LORD, hear my prayer; hearken to my pleading in your faithfulness; in your justice answer me. And enter not into judgment with your servant, for before you no living man is just. For the enemy pursues me; he has crushed my life to the ground; he has left me dwelling in the dark, like those long dead. And my spirit is faint within me; my heart within me is appalled. I remember the days of old; I meditate on all your doings, your work of your hands I ponder. I stretch out my hands to you; my soul thirsts for you like parched land. Hasten to answer me O LORD, for my spirit fails me. Hide not your face from me lest I become like those who go down into the pit. At dawn let me hear of your kindness for in you I trust. Show me the way in which I should walk, for to you I lift up my soul. Rescue me from my enemies, O LORD, for in you I hope. Teach me to do your will, for you are my God. May your good spirit guide me on level ground. For your name's sake, O LORD, preserve me; in your justice free me from distress, and in your kindness destroy my enemies; bring to naught all my foes, for I am your servant.

Psalms for the Stressed and Afflicted

Psalm 143(144): 1-8
Blessed be the LORD, my rock, who trains my hands for battle, my fingers for war; my refuge and my fortress, my stronghold, my deliverer, my shield in whom I trust, who subdues people under me. LORD what is man, that you notice him; the son of man, that you take thought of him? Man is like a breath; his days, like a passing shadow. Incline your heavens, O LORD, and come down; touch the mountains and they shall smoke; flash forth lightening, and put them to flight, shoot your arrows and rout them; reach out your hand from on high—deliver me and rescue me from many waters, from the hands of aliens, whose mouths swear false promises while their right hands are raised in perjury.

Words of Comfort

Psalms, Words of Comfort

Psalm 3:3-7
Many are saying of me, "There is no salvation for him in God." But you, O LORD are my shield; my glory, you lift up my head!
When I call out to the LORD, he answers me from his holy mountain.
When I lie down in sleep, I wake again for the LORD sustains me.
I fear not the myriads of people arrayed against me on every side.

Psalm 4:8-9
You put gladness into my heart, more than when grain and wine abound.
As soon as I lie down, I fall peacefully asleep, for you alone, O LORD, bring security to my dwelling.

Psalm 9A:10-11
The LORD is a stronghold for the oppressed, a stronghold in time of distress.
They trust in you who cherish your name, for you forsake not those who seek you O LORD.

Psalm 17(18):31
God's way is unerring, the promise of the LORD is fire-tried; he is a shield to all who take refuge in him.

Psalm 21(22):27
The lowly shall eat their fill; they who seek the LORD shall praise him; "May your hearts be ever merry!"

Psalms, Words of Comfort

Psalm 22(23):1-6
The LORD is my shepherd; I shall not want.
In Verdant pastures he gives me repose; besides restful waters he leads me; he refreshes my soul.
He guides me in right paths for his name's sake.
Even though I walk in the dark valley I fear no evil; for you are at my side with your rod and staff that give me courage.
You spread the table before me in the sight of my foes; you anoint my head with oil; my cup overflows.
Only goodness and kindness follow me all the days of my life; and I shall dwell in the house of the LORD for years to come.

Psalm 27(28):6-7
Blessed be the LORD for he has heard the sound of my pleading; the LORD is my strength and my shield; in him my heart rests, and I find help; then my heart exults, and with my song I give him thanks.

Psalm 29(30):3-4, 12-13
O LORD, my God, I cried out to you and you healed me.
O LORD, you brought me up from the nether world; you preserved me from among those going down into the pit.
You changed my mourning into dancing; you took off my sackcloth and clothed me with gladness, that

my soul might sing praise to you without ceasing; O LORD, my God, forever will I give you thanks.

Psalm 30(31):4-8, 20, 22-23
You are my rock and my fortress; for your name's sake you will lead and guide me.
You will free me, from the snare they set for me, for you are my refuge.
Into your hands I commend my spirit; you will redeem me, O LORD, O faithful God.
You hate those who worship vain idols, but my trust is in the LORD.
I will rejoice and be glad of your kindness, when you have seen my affliction and watched over me in my distress.
How great is the goodness, O LORD, which you have in store for those who fear you, and which, toward those who take refuge in you, you show in the sight of men.
Blessed be the LORD whose wondrous kindness he has shown me in a fortified city.
Once I said in my anguish, "I am cut off from your sight" yet you heard the sound of my pleading when I cried out to you.

Psalm 31(32):1-2, 8
Happy is he whose fault is taken away, whose sin is covered.
Happy the man to whom the LORD imputes not guilt, in whose spirit there is no guile.

Psalms, Words of Comfort

I will instruct you and show you the way you should walk; I will counsel you, keeping my eye on you.

Psalm 33(34):1-11, 18-23
I will bless the LORD at all times; his praise shall be ever in my mouth.
Let my soul glory in the LORD; the lowly will hear me and be glad.
Glorify the LORD with me, let us together extol his name.
I sought the LORD, and he answered me and delivered me from all my fears.
Look to him that you may be radiant with joy, and your faces may not blush with shame.
When the afflicted man called out, the LORD heard him, and from all his distress he saved him.
The angel of the LORD encamps around those who fear him, and delivers them.
Taste and see how good the LORD is; happy the man who takes refuge in him.
Fear the LORD, you his holy ones, for naught is lacking to those who fear him.
The great grow poor and hungry; but those who seek the LORD want for no good thing.
When the just cry out, the LORD hears them, and from all their distress he rescues them.
The LORD is close to the brokenhearted; and those who are crushed in spirit he saves.
Many are the troubles of the just man, but out of them all the LORD delivers him; he watches over all his bones; not one of them shall be broken.

Psalms, Words of Comfort

Vice slays the wicked, and the enemies of the just pay for their guilt.
But the LORD redeems the lives of his servants; no one incurs guilt who takes refuge in him.

Psalm 35(36):6-10
O LORD, your kindness reaches to heaven; your faithfulness, to the clouds.
Your justice is like the mountains of God; your judgments, like the mighty deep; man and beast you save, O LORD.
How precious is your kindness, O God! The children of men take refuge in the shadow of your wings.
They have their fill of the prime gifts of your house; from your delightful stream you give them to drink.
For with you is the fountain of life, and in your light we see light.

Psalm 39(40):A1-4
I have waited, waited for the LORD, and he stooped toward me and heard my cry.
He drew me out of the pit of destruction, out of the mud of the swamp; he set my feet upon a crag; he made firm my steps.
And he put a new song into my mouth, a hymn to our God. Many shall look on in awe and trust in the LORD.

Psalms, Words of Comfort

Psalm 45(46):1-4 5-6, 9-11
God is our refuge and our strength, an ever-present help in distress.
Therefore we fear not, though the earth be shaken and mountains plunge into the depths of the sea; though its waters rage and foam and the mountains quake at its surging.
There is a stream whose runlets gladden the city of God, the holy dwelling of the Most High.
God is in its midst; it shall not be disturbed; God will help it at the break of dawn.
Come! Behold the deeds of the LORD, the astounding things he has wrought on earth; he has stopped wars to the end of the earth; the bow he breaks; he splinters the spears; he burns the shields with fire.
Desist! And confess that I am God, exalted among the nations, exalted upon the earth.

Psalm 46(47):1-3, 6-9
All you peoples, clap your hands, shout to God with cries of gladness, for the LORD, the Most High, the awesome, is the great king over all the earth.
God mounts his throne amid shouts of joy; the LORD, amid trumpet blasts.
Sing praise to God, sing praise; sing praise to our king, sing praise.
For king of all the earth is God; sing hymns of praise.
God reigns over the nations, God sits upon his holy throne.

Psalms, Words of Comfort

Psalm 54(55):23
Cast your care upon the LORD, and he will support you; never will he permit the just man to be disturbed.

Psalm 61(62):1-3, 6-13
Only in God is my soul at rest; from him comes my salvation.
He only is my rock and my salvation, my stronghold; I shall not be disturbed at all.
Only in God be at rest, my soul, for from him comes my hope.
He only is my rock and my salvation, my stronghold; I shall not be disturbed.
With God is my safety and my glory, he is the rock of my strength; my refuge is in God.
Trust in him at all times, O my people! Pour out your hearts before him; God is our refuge.
Only a breath are mortal men; an illusion are men of rank; in a balance they prove lighter, all together, than a breath.
Trust not in extortion; in plunder take no empty pride; though wealth abound, set not your heart upon it.
One thing God said; these two things which I heard; that power belongs to God, and yours, O LORD, is kindness; and that you render to everyone according to his deeds.

Psalms, Words of Comfort

Psalm 62 (63):1-9
O God, you are my God whom I seek; for you my flesh pines and my soul thirsts like the earth, parched, lifeless and without water.
Thus have I gazed toward you in the sanctuary to see your power and your glory, for your kindness is a greater good than life; my lips shall glorify you.
Thus have I bless you while I live; lifting up my hands, I will call upon your name.
As with the riches of a banquet shall my soul be satisfied, and with exultant lips my mouth shall praise you.
I will remember you upon my couch, and through the night-watches I will meditate on you: that you are my help, and in the shadow of your wings I shout for joy.
My soul clings fast to you; your right hand upholds me.

Psalm 63(64):11
The just man is glad in the LORD and takes refuge in him; in him glory all the upright of heart.

Psalm 64(65):1-14
To you we owe our hymn of praise, O God, in Sion; to you must vows be fulfilled, you who hear prayers.
To you all flesh must come because of wicked deeds.
We are overcome by our sins; it is you who pardon them.

Psalms, Words of Comfort

Happy the man you choose, and bring to dwell in your courts.
May we be filled with the good things of your house, the holy things of your temple!
With awe-inspiring deeds of justice you answer us, O God our savior, the hope of all the ends of the earth and of the distant seas.
You set the mountains in place by your power, you who are girt with might; you still the roaring of seas, the roaring of their waves and the tumult of the peoples.
And the dwellers at the earth's ends are in fear at your marvels; the farthest east and west you make resound with joy.
You have visited the land and watered it; greatly have you enriched it.
God's watercourses are filled; you have prepared the grain.
Thus have you prepared the land: drenching its furrows, breaking up its clods, softening it with showers, blessing its yield.
You have crowned the year with your bounty, and your paths overflow with a rich harvest; the untilled meadows overflow with it, and rejoicing clothes the hills.
The fields are garmented with flocks and the valleys blanketed with grain. They shout and sing for joy.

Psalms, Words of Comfort

Psalm 65(66):16-20
Hear now, all you who fear God, while I declare what he has done for me.
When I appealed to him in words, praise was on the tip of my tongue.
Were I to cherish wickedness in my heart, the LORD would not hear; but God has heard; he has hearkened to the sound of my prayer.
Blessed be God who refuses me not my prayer or his kindness!

Psalm 66(67):1-8
May God have pity on us and bless us; may he let his face shine upon us.
So may your way be known upon earth; among all nations, your salvation.
May the peoples praise you, O God; may all the peoples praise you!
May the nations be glad and exult because you rule the peoples in equity; the nations on the earth you guide.
May the peoples praise you, O God; may all the peoples praise you!
The earth has yielded its fruits; God, our God, has blessed us.
May God bless us, and may all the ends of the earth fear him!

Psalm 67(68):1-7, 10-12, 20, 21
God arises; his enemies are scattered, and those who hate him flee before him.

Psalms, Words of Comfort

As smoke is driven away, so are they driven; as wax melts before the fire, so the wicked perish before God.
But the just rejoice and exult before God; they are glad and rejoice.
Sing to God, chant praise to his name, extol him who rides upon the clouds, whose name is the LORD; exult before him.
The father of orphans and the defender of widows is God in his holy dwelling.
God gives a home to the forsaken; he leads forth prisoners to prosperity; only rebels remain in the parched land.
A bountiful rain you showered down, O God, upon your inheritance; you restored the land when it languished; your flock settled in it; in your goodness, O God, you provided it for the needy.
The LORD gives the word; women bear the glad tidings, a vast army.
Blessed day by day be the LORD, who bears our burdens; God, who is our salvation.
God is a saving God for us; the LORD, my LORD, controls the passageways of death.

Psalms 68(69):33-34
"See, you lowly ones, and be glad; you who seek God, may your hearts be merry!
For the LORD hears the poor, and his own who are in bonds he spurns not.

Psalms, Words of Comfort

Psalm 85(86):8-10
There's none like you among the gods, O LORD, and there are no works like yours.
All the nations you have made shall come and worship you, O LORD, and glorify your name.
For you are great, and you do wondrous deeds; you alone are God.

Psalm 88(89):1-3, 6-10, 12, 14-18
The favors of the LORD I will sing forever; through all generations my mouth shall proclaim your faithfulness.
For you have said, "My kindness is established forever": in heaven you have confirmed your faithfulness:"
The heavens proclaim your wonders, O LORD, and your faithfulness, in the assembly of the holy ones.
For who in the skies can rank with the LORD?
Who is like the LORD among the sons of God?
God is terrible in the council of the holy ones; he is great and awesome beyond all round about him.
O LORD, God of hosts, who is like you? Mighty are you, O LORD, and your faithfulness surrounds you.
You rule over the surging of the sea, you still the swelling of its waves.
Yours is a mighty arm; strong is your hand, exalted hand.
Justice and judgment are the foundation of your throne; kindness and truth go before you.
Happy the people who know the joyful shout; in the light of your countenance, O LORD, they walk.

Psalms, Words of Comfort

At your name they rejoice all the day, and through your justice they are exalted.
For you are the splendor of their strength, and by your favor our horn is exalted.

Psalm 93(94):18-19
When I say "My foot is slipping," your kindness, O LORD, sustains me; when cares abound within me, your comfort gladdens my soul.

Psalm 137(138):7, 8
Though I walk amid distress, you preserve me; against the anger of my enemies you raise your hand; your right hand saves me.
The LORD will complete what he has done for me; your kindness, O LORD, endures forever; forsake not the work of your hands.

Psalm 138(139):1-24
O LORD, you have probed me and you know me; you know when I sit and when I stand; you understand my thoughts from afar.
My journeys and my rest you scrutinize, with all my ways you are familiar.
Even before a word is on my tongue, behold, O LORD, you know the whole of it.
Behind me and before, you hem me in and rest your hand upon me.
Such knowledge is too wonderful for me; too lofty for me to attain.
Where can I go from your spirit? From your presence where can I flee?

Psalms, Words of Comfort

If I go up to the heavens, you are there; if I sink to the nether world, you are present there.
If I take the wings of the dawn, if I settle at the farthest limits of the sea, even there your hand shall guide me, and your right hand hold me fast.
If I say, "Surely the darkness shall hide me, and night shall be my light"– for you darkness itself is not dark, and night shines as the day. [Darkness and light are the same.]
Truly you have formed my inmost being; you knit me in my mother's womb.
I give you thanks that I am fearfully, wonderfully made; wonderful are your works.
My soul also you knew full well; nor was my frame unknown to you when I was made in secret, when I was fashioned in the depths of the earth.
Your eyes have seen my actions; in your book they are all written; my days were limited before one of them existed.
How weighty are your designs, O God; how vast the sum of them!
Were I to recount them, they would outnumber the sands; did I reach the end of them, I should still be with you.
If only you would destroy the wicked, O God, and the men of blood were to depart from me!
Wickedly they invoke your name; your foes swear faithless oaths.
Do I not hate, O LORD, those who hate you? Those who rise up against you do I not loathe?
With a deadly hatred I hate them; they are my enemies.

Psalms, Words of Comfort

Prove me, O God, and know my heart; try me, and know my thoughts; see if my way is crooked, and lead me in the way of old.

Psalm 144(145):1-21
I will extol you, O my God and King, and I will bless your name forever and ever.
Every day will I bless you and I will praise your name forever and ever.
Great is the LORD and highly to be praised; his greatness is unsearchable.
Generation after generation praises your works and proclaims your might.
They speak of the splendor of your glorious majesty and tell of your wondrous works.
They discourse of the power of your terrible deed and declare your greatness.
They publish the fame of your abundant goodness and joyfully sing of your justice.
The LORD is gracious and merciful, slow to anger and of great kindness.
The LORD is good to all and compassionate toward all his works.
Let all your works give you thanks, O LORD, and let your faithful ones bless you.
Let them discourse of the glory of your kingdom and speak of your might, making known to men your might and the glorious splendor of your kingdom.
Your kingdom is a kingdom for all ages, and your dominion endures through all generations.

Psalms, Words of Comfort

The LORD is faithful in all his words and holy in all his works.
The LORD lifts up all who are falling and raises up all who are bowed down.
The eyes of all look hopefully to you, and you give them their food in due season; you open your hand and satisfy the desire of every living thing.
The LORD is just in all his ways and holy in all his works.
The LORD is near to all who call upon him, to all who call upon him in truth.
He fulfills the desire of those who fear him, he hears their cry and saves them.
The LORD keeps all who love him, but all the wicked he will destroy.
May my mouth speak the praise of the LORD, and may all flesh bless his holy name forever and ever.

Words of Praise & Wisdom

Psalms, Words of Praise and Wisdom

Psalm 18(19):8-11
The law of the LORD is perfect, refreshing the soul; the decree of the LORD is trustworthy, giving wisdom to the simple.
The percepts of the LORD are right, rejoicing the heart; the command of the LORD is clear, enlightening the eye; the fear of the LORD is pure, enduring forever; the ordinances of the LORD are true, all of them just; they are more precious than gold, than a heap of purest gold; sweeter also than syrup or honey from the comb.

Psalm 23(24):3-5
Who can ascend the mountain of the LORD? Or who may stand in his holy place?
He whose hands are sinless, whose heart is clean, who desires not what is vain, nor swears deceitfully to his neighbor; he shall receive a blessing from the LORD, a reward from God his savior.

Psalm 24(25):12-15
When a man fears the LORD, he shows him the way he should choose.
He abides in prosperity, and his descendants inherit the land.
The friendship of the LORD is with those who fear him, and his covenant, for their instruction.
My eyes are ever toward the LORD, for he will free my feet from the snare.

Psalms, Words of Praise and Wisdom

Psalm 28(29):1-2
Give to the LORD, you sons of God, give to the LORD glory and praise, give to the LORD the glory due his name; adore the LORD in holy attire.

Psalm 29(30):5-10
Sing praise to the LORD, you his faithful ones, and give thanks to his holy name.
For his anger lasts but a moment; a lifetime, his good will. At nightfall, weeping enters in, but with the dawn, rejoicing.
Once, in my security, I said, "I shall never be disturbed."
O LORD, in your goodwill you have endowed me with majesty and strength; but when you hid your face I was terrified.
To you, O LORD, I cried out; with the LORD I pleaded: "What gain would there be from my lifeblood, from my going down into the grave? Would dust give you thanks or proclaim your faithfulness?"

Psalm 30(31):24, 25
Love the LORD, all you his faithful ones! The LORD keeps those who are constant, but more than requites those who act proudly. Take courage and be stouthearted, all you who hope in the LORD.

Psalms, Words of Praise and Wisdom

Psalm 32(33):1-5, 8-19, 22
Exult, you just, in the LORD; praise from the upright is fitting.
Give thanks to the LORD on the harp; with a ten stringed lyre chant his praises.
Sing to him a new song; pluck the strings skillfully, with shouts of gladness. For upright is the word of the LORD, and all his works are trustworthy.
He loves justice and right; of the kindness of the LORD the earth is full.
Let all the earth fear the LORD; let all who dwell in the world revere him. For he spoke and it was made; he commanded, and it stood forth.
The LORD brings to naught the plans of nations; he foils the design of peoples. But the plans of the LORD stands forever; the design of his heart, through all generations.
Happy the nation whose God is the LORD, the people he has chosen for his own inheritance.
From heaven the LORD looks down; he sees all mankind.
From his fixed throne he beholds all who dwell on the earth.
He who fashioned the heart of each, he who knows all their works.
A king is not saved by a mighty army, nor is a warrior delivered by great strength. Useless is the horse for safety; great though its strength, it cannot provide escape. But see, the eyes of the LORD are upon those who fear him, upon those who hope for his kindness, to deliver them from death and preserve them in spite of famine.

Psalms, Words of Praise and Wisdom

May your kindness, O LORD, be upon us who have put our hope in you.

Psalm 38(39):1-14
I said "I will watch my ways, so as not to sin with my tongue; I will set a curb on my mouth." While the wicked man was before me I kept dumb and silent; I refrained from rash speech. But my grief was stirred up: hot grew my heart within me; in my thoughts, a fire blazed forth. I spoke out with my tongue: Let me know, O LORD, my end and what is the number of my days, that I may learn how frail I am. A short span you have made my days, and my life is as naught before you; only a breath is any human existence. A phantom only, man goes his ways; like vapor only are his restless pursuits; he heaps up stores, and knows not who will use them. And now, for what do I wait, O LORD? In you is my hope. From all my sins deliver me; a fool's taunt let me not suffer.
I was speechless and opened not my mouth, because it was your doing; take away your scourge from me; at the blow of your hand I wasted away. With rebukes for guilt you chasten man; you dissolve like a cobweb all that is dear to him; only a breath is any man. Hear my prayer, O LORD; to my cry give ear; to my weeping be not deaf! For I am but a wayfarer before you, a pilgrim like all my fathers. Turn your gaze from me, that I may find respite ere I depart and be no more.

Psalms, Words of Praise and Wisdom

Psalm 39(40):5-11
Happy the man who makes the LORD his trust; who turns not to idolatry or to those who stray after falsehood.
How numerous have you made, O LORD, my God, your wondrous deeds! And in your plans for us there is none to equal you; should I wish to declare or to tell them, they would be too many to recount. Sacrifice or oblation you wished not, but ears open to obedience you gave me. Holocausts or sin-offerings you sought not; then said I, "Behold I come; in the written scroll it is prescribed for me, to do your will, O my God, is my delight, and your law is within my heart!" I announce your justice in the vast assembly; I did not restrain my lips, as you, O LORD, know.
Your justice I kept not hid within my heart; your faithfulness and your salvation I have spoken of; I have made no secret of your kindness and your truth in the vast assembly.

Psalm 40(41):1-4
Happy is he who has regard for the lowly and the poor; in the day of misfortune the LORD will deliver him.
The LORD will keep and preserve him; he will make him happy on the earth, and not give him over to the will of his enemies. The LORD will help him on his sickbed, he will take away all his ailment when he is ill.

Psalms, Words of Praise and Wisdom

Psalm 48(49):1-21
Hear this, all you peoples; hearken, all who dwell in the world, of lowly birth or high degree, rich and poor alike. My mouth shall speak wisdom; prudence shall be the utterance of my heart. My ear is intent upon a proverb; I will set forth my riddle to the music of the harp. Why should I fear in evil days when my wicked ensnarers ring me round? They trust in their wealth; the abundance of their riches is their boast. Yet in no way can a man redeem himself, or pay his own ransom to God; too high is the price to redeem one's life; he would never have enough to remain alive always and not see destruction. For he can see that wise men die, and likewise the senseless and the stupid pass away, leaving to others their wealth. Tombs are their homes forever, their dwellings through all generations, though they have called lands in their names. Thus man, for all his splendor, does not abide; he resembles the beasts that perish. This the way of those whose trust is folly, the end of those contented with their lot: Like sheep they are herded into the nether world; death is their shepherd, and the upright rule over them. Quickly their form is consumed; the nether world is their palace. But God will redeem me from the power of the nether world by receiving me. Fear not when a man grows rich, when the wealth of his house becomes great, for when he dies, he shall take none of it; his wealth shall not follow him down. Though in his lifetime he counted himself blessed, "They will praise you for doing well for yourself," he shall join the circle

Psalms, Words of Praise and Wisdom

of his forebears who shall never more see light. Man, for all his splendor, if he have not prudence, resembles the beasts that perish.

Psalm 49(50):14-15
Offer to God praise as your sacrifice and fulfill your vows to the Most High; then call upon me in time of distress; I will rescue you, and you shall glorify me."

Psalm 65(66):1-9
Shout joyfully to God, all you on earth, sing praise to the glory of his name; proclaim his glorious praise. Say to God, "How tremendous are your deeds! For your great strength your enemies fawn upon you. Let all on earth worship and sing praise to you, sing praise to your name!" Come and see the works of God, his tremendous deeds among men. He has changed the sea into dry land; through the river they passed on foot; therefore let us rejoice in him. He rules by his might forever; his eyes watch the nations; rebels may not exalt themselves. Bless our God, you peoples, loudly sound his praise; he has given life to our souls, and has not let our feet slip.

Psalm 74(75):1-9
We give you thanks, O God, we give thanks, and we invoke your name; we declare your wondrous deeds. "When I seized the appointed time, I will judge with equity. Though the earth and all who dwell in it quake, I have set firm its pillars. I say to

Psalms, Words of Praise and Wisdom

the boastful: Boast not; and to the wicked: Lift not up your horns." Lift not up your horns against the Most High; speak not haughtily against the Rock. For neither from the east nor from the west, neither from the desert nor from the mountains— But God is the judge; one he brings low; another he lifts up.

Psalm 77(78):1-4, 6-8
Hearken, my people, to my teaching; incline your ears to the words of my mouth. I will open my mouth in a parable, I will utter mysteries from of old. What we have heard and know, and what our fathers have declared to us, we will not hide from their sons; we will declare to the generation to come the glorious deeds of the LORD and his strength and the wonders that he wrought. So that the generations to come might know, their sons yet to be born, that they too may rise and declare to their sons that they should put their hope in God, and not forget the deeds of God but keep his commands, and not be like their fathers, a generation wayward and rebellious: a generation that kept not its heart steadfast nor its spirit faithful toward God.

Psalm 92(93):1-5
The LORD is king, in splendor robed; robed is the LORD and girt about with strength; and he has made the world firm, not to be moved. Your throne stands firm from of old; from everlasting you are, O LORD. The floods lift up, O LORD, the floods lift their voice; the floods lift up their tumult. More powerful than the roar of many waters, more

Psalms, Words of Praise and Wisdom

powerful than the breakers of the sea— powerful on high is the LORD. Your decrees are worthy of trust indeed; holiness befits your house, O LORD, for length of days.

Psalm 94(95):1-7
Come, let us sing joyfully to the LORD; let us acclaim the rock of our salvation. Let us greet him with thanksgiving; let us joyfully sing psalms to him. For the LORD is a great God, and a great king above all gods; in his hands are the depths of the earth, and the tops of the mountains are his. His is the sea, for he has made it, and the dry land, which his hands have formed. Come, let us bow down in worship; let us kneel before the LORD who made us. For he is our God, and we are the people he shepherds, the flock he guides.

Psalm 95(96):1-13
Sing to the LORD a new song; sing to the LORD, all you lands. Sing to the LORD; bless his name; announce his salvation, day after day. Tell his glory among the nations; among all peoples his wondrous deeds. For great is the LORD and highly to be praised; awesome is he, beyond all gods. For all the gods of the nations are things of naught, but the LORD made the heavens. Splendor and majesty go before him; praise and grandeur are in his sanctuary. Give to the LORD, you families of nations, give to the LORD glory and praise; give to the LORD the glory due his name! Bring gifts, and enter his courts; worship the LORD in holy attire.

Psalms, Words of Praise and Wisdom

Tremble before him, all the earth; say among the nations: the LORD is king. He has made the world firm, not to be moved; he governs the peoples with equity. Let the heavens be glad and the earth rejoice; let the sea and what fills it resound; let the plains be joyful and all that is in them! Then shall all the trees of the forest exult before the LORD, for he comes; for he comes to rule the earth. He shall rule the world with justice and the peoples with his constancy.

Psalm 96(97):1-7, 9-12
The LORD is king; let the earth rejoice; let the many isles be glad. Clouds and darkness are round about him, justice and judgment are the foundation of his throne. Fire goes before him and consumes his foes round about. His lightnings illumine the world; the earth sees and trembles. The mountains melt like wax before the LORD, before the LORD of all the earth. The heavens proclaim his justice, and all peoples see his glory. All who worship graven things are put to shame, who glory in the things of naught; all gods are prostrate before him. Because you, O LORD, are the Most High over all the earth, exalted far above all gods. The LORD loves those that hate evil; he guards the lives of his faithful ones; from the hand of the wicked he delivers them. Light dawns for the just; and gladness, for the upright of heart. Be glad in the LORD, you just, and give thanks to his holy name.

Psalms, Words of Praise and Wisdom

Psalms 97(98):1-2, 4-9
Sing to the LORD a new song, for he has done wondrous deeds; his right hand has won victory for him, his holy arm. The LORD has made his salvation known: in the sight of the nations he has revealed his justice. Sing joyfully to the LORD, all you lands; break into song; sing praise. Sing praise to the LORD with the harp, with the harp and melodious song. With trumpets and the sound of the horn sing joyfully before the King, the LORD. Let the sea and what fills it resound, the world and those who dwell in it; let the rivers clap their hands, the mountains shout with them for joy before the LORD, for he comes, for he comes to rule the earth; he will rule the world with justice and the peoples with equity.

Psalm 99(100):1-5
Sing joyfully to the LORD, all you lands; serve the LORD with gladness; come before him with joyful song. Know that the LORD is God; he made us, his we are; his people, the flock he tends. Enter his gates with thanksgiving, his courts with praise; give thanks to him; bless his name, for he is good: the LORD, whose kindness endures forever, and his faithfulness to all generations.

Psalms, Words of Praise and Wisdom

Psalm 102(103):1-6, 8-22
Bless the LORD, O my soul; and all my being, bless his holy name. Bless the LORD, O my soul, and forget not all his benefits; he pardons all your iniquities, he heals all your ills. He redeems your life from destruction, he crowns you with kindness and compassion. He fills your lifetime with good; your youth is renewed like the eagle's. The LORD secures justice and the rights of all the oppressed. Merciful and gracious is the LORD, slow to anger and abounding in kindness. He will not always chide, nor does he keep his wrath forever. Not according to our sins does he deal with us, nor does he requite us according to our crimes. For as the heavens are high above the earth so surpassing is his kindness toward those who fear him. As far as the east is from the west, so far has he put our transgressions from us. As a father has compassion on his children, so the LORD has compassion on those who fear him. For he knows how we are formed; he remembers that we are dust. Man's days are like those of grass; like a flower of the field he blooms; the wind sweeps over him and he is gone, and his place knows him no more. But the kindness of the LORD is from eternity to eternity toward those who fear him, and his justice toward children's children among those who keep his covenant and remember to fulfill his precepts. The LORD has established his throne in heaven, and his kingdom rules over all. Bless the LORD, all you his angels, you mighty in strength, who do his bidding, obeying his spoken word. Bless the

Psalms, Words of Praise and Wisdom

LORD, all you his hosts, his ministers, who do his will. Bless the LORD, all his works, everywhere in his domain. Bless the LORD, O my soul!

Psalm 103(104): 1-35
Bless the LORD, O my soul! O LORD, my God, you are great indeed! You are clothed with majesty and glory, robed in light as with a cloak. You have spread out the heavens like a tentcloth; you have constructed your palace upon the waters. You make the clouds your chariot; you travel on the wings of the wind. You make the winds your messengers, and flaming fire your ministers. You fixed the earth upon its foundation, not be moved forever; with the ocean, as with a garment, you covered it; above the mountains the waters stood. At your rebuke they fled, at the sound of your thunder they took flight; as the mountains rose, they went down the valleys to the place you had fixed for them. You set a limit they may not pass, nor shall they cover the earth again. You send forth springs into the watercourses that wind among the mountains, and give drink to every beast of the field, till the wild asses quench their thirst. Beside them the birds of heaven dwell; from among the branches they send forth their song. You water the mountains from your palace; the earth is replete with the fruit of your works. You raise the grass for the cattle, and vegetation for men's use, producing bread from the earth, and wine to gladden men's hearts, that their faces gleam with oil, and bread fortifies the hearts of men. Well watered are the trees of the LORD, the cedars of

Psalms, Words of Praise and Wisdom

Lebanon, which he planted; in them the birds build their nests; fir trees are the home of the stork. The high mountains are for wild goats; the cliffs are a refuge for rock-badgers. You made the moon to mark the seasons; the suns knows the hour of its setting. You bring darkness, and it is night; then all the beasts of the forest roam about; young lions roar for the prey and seek their food from God. When the sun rises, they withdraw and couch in their dens. Man goes forth to his work and to his tillage till the evening. How manifold are your works, O LORD! In wisdom you have wrought them all— the earth is full of your creatures; the sea also, great and wide, in which are schools without number of living things both small and great, and where ships move about with Leviathan, which you formed to make sport of it. They all look to you to give them food in due time. When you give it to them, they gather it; when you open your hand, they are filled with good things. If you hide your face, they are dismayed; if you take away their breath, they perish and return to their dust. When you send forth your spirit, they are created, and you renew the face of the earth. May the glory of the LORD endure forever; may the LORD be glad in his works! He who looks upon the earth, and it trembles; who touches the mountains, and they smoke! I will sing to the LORD all my life; I will sing praise to my God while I live. Pleasing to him be my theme; I will be glad in the LORD. May sinners cease from the earth, and may the wicked be no more. Bless the LORD, O my soul! Alleluia.

Psalms, Words of Praise and Wisdom

Psalm 104 (105):1-4
Give Thanks to the LORD, invoke his name; make known among the nations his deeds. Sing to him, sing his praise, proclaim all his wondrous deeds. Glory in his holy name; rejoice, O hearts that seek the LORD. Look to the LORD in his strength; seek to serve him constantly.

Psalm 105(106):1-5
Give thanks to the LORD, for he is good, for his kindness endures forever. Who can tell the mighty deeds of the LORD, or proclaim all his praises? Happy are they who observe what is right, who do always what is just. Remember me, O LORD, as you favor your people; visit me with your saving help, that I may see the prosperity of your chosen ones, rejoice in the joy of your people, and glory with your inheritance.

Psalm 106(107): 1
Give thanks to the LORD, for he is good, for his kindness endures forever!

Psalm 107(108):1-7
My heart is steadfast, O God; my heart is steadfast; I will sing and chant praise. Awake, O my soul; awake, lyre and harp; I will wake the dawn. I will give thanks to you among the peoples, O LORD; I will chant your praise among the nations. For your kindness towers to the heavens, and your faithfulness to the skies. Be exalted above the

Psalms, Words of Praise and Wisdom

heavens, O God; over the heavens, O God; over all the earth be your glory! That your loved ones may escape, help us by your right hand, and answer us.

Psalm 110(111):1-10
I will give thanks to the LORD with all my heart in the company and the assembly of the just. Great are the works of the LORD, exquisite in all their delights. Majesty and glory are his work, and his justice endures forever. He has won renown for his wondrous deeds; gracious and merciful is the LORD. He has given food to those who fear him; he will forever be mindful of his covenant. He has made known to his people the power of his works, giving them the inheritance of the nations. The works of his hands are faithful and just; sure are all his percepts. Reliable forever and ever, wrought in truth and equity. He has sent deliverance to his people; he has ratified his covenant forever; holy and awesome is his name. The fear of the LORD is the beginning of wisdom; prudent are all who live by it. His praise endures forever.

Psalm 111(112):1-10
Happy the man who fears the LORD, who greatly delights in his commands. His posterity shall be mighty upon the earth; the upright generation shall be blessed. Wealth and riches shall be in his house; his generosity shall endure forever. He dawns through the darkness, a light for the upright; he is gracious and merciful and just. Well for the man who is gracious and lends, who conducts his affairs

Psalms, Words of Praise and Wisdom

with justice; he shall never be moved; the just man shall be in everlasting remembrance. An evil report he shall not fear; his heart is firm, trusting in the LORD. His heart is steadfast; he shall not fear till he looks down upon his foes. Lavishly he gives to the poor; his generosity shall endure forever; his horn shall be exalted in glory. The wicked man shall see it and be vexed; he shall gnash his teeth and pine away; the desire of the wicked shall perish.

Psalm 112(113):1-9
Praise, you servants of the LORD, praise the name of the LORD. Blessed be the name of the LORD both now and forever. From the rising to the setting of the sun is the name of the LORD to be praised. High above all nations is the LORD; above the heavens is his glory. Who is like the LORD, our God, who is enthroned on high and looks upon the heavens and the earth below? He raises up the lowly from the dust; from the dunghill he lifts up the poor to seat them with princes, with the princes of his own people. He establishes in her home the barren wife as the joyful mother of children.

Psalm 113B(115):1,11, 13-18
Not to us, O LORD, not to us but to your name give glory because of your kindness, because of your truth. Those who fear the LORD trust in the LORD; he is their help and their shield. He will bless those who fear the LORD, both the small and the great. May the LORD bless you more and more, both you and your children. May you be

blessed by the LORD, who made heaven and earth. Heaven is the heaven of the LORD, but the earth he has given to the children of men. It is not the dead who praise the LORD, nor those who go down into silence; but we bless the LORD, both now and forever.

Psalm 114(116A):1-9
I love the LORD because he has heard my voice in supplication, because he has inclined his ear to me the day I called. The cords of death encompassed me; the snares of the nether world seized upon me; I fell into distress and sorrow, and I called upon the name of the LORD, "O LORD save my life!" Gracious is the LORD and just; yes, our God is merciful. The LORD keeps the little ones; I was brought low, and he saved me. Return, O my soul, to your tranquility, for the LORD has been good to you. For he has freed my soul from death, my eyes from tears, my feet from stumbling. I shall walk before the LORD in the lands of the living.

Psalm 116(117):1-2
Praise the LORD, all you nations; glorify him, all you peoples! For steadfast is his kindness toward us, and the fidelity of the LORD endures forever.

Psalms, Words of Praise and Wisdom

Psalm 117(118):1, 4-8, 13-14, 19-29
Give thanks to the LORD, for he is good, for his mercy endures forever. Let those who fear the LORD say, "His mercy endures forever." In my straits I called upon the LORD; the LORD answered me and set me free. The LORD is with me; I fear not; what can man do against me? The LORD is with me to help me, and I shall look down upon my foes. It is better to take refuge in the LORD than to trust in man. I was hard pressed and was falling, but the LORD helped me. My strength and my courage is the LORD, and he has been my savior. Open to me the gates of justice; I will enter them and give thanks to the LORD. This gate is the LORD'S; the just shall enter it. I will give thanks to you, for you have answered me and have been my savior. The stone which the builders rejected has become the cornerstone. By the LORD has this been done; it is wonderful in our eyes. This is the day the LORD has made; let us be glad and rejoice in it. O LORD, grant salvation! O LORD, grant prosperity! Blessed is he who comes in the name of the LORD; we bless you from the house of the LORD. The LORD is God, and he has given us light. Join in procession with leafy boughs up to the horns of the altar. You are my God, and I give thanks to you; O my God, I extol you. Give thanks to the LORD, for he is good; for his kindness endures forever.

Psalms, Words of Praise and Wisdom

Psalm 118(119):1-56, 57-83, 89-120, 123-132, 135-144,, 162-176
Happy are they whose way is blameless, who walk in the law of the LORD. Happy are they who observe his decrees, who seek him with all their heart, and do no wrong, but walk in his ways. You have commanded that your precepts be diligently kept. Oh, that I might be firm in the ways of keeping your statutes! Then should I not be put to shame when I beheld all your commands. I will give you thanks with an upright heart, when I have learned your just ordinances. I will keep your statues; do not utterly forsake me. How shall a young man be faultless in his way? By keeping to your words. With all my heart I seek you; let me not stray from your commands. Within my heart I treasure your promise, that I may not sin against you. Blessed are you, O LORD; teach me your statues. With my lips I declare all the ordinances of your mouth. In the way of your decrees I rejoice, as much as in all riches. I will meditate on your precepts, and consider your ways. In your statues I will delight; I will not forget your words. Be good to your servant, that I mat live and keep your words. Open my eyes, that I may consider the wonders of your law. I am a wayfarer of earth; hide not your commands from me. My soul is consumed with longing for your ordinances at all times. You rebuke the accursed proud, who turn away from your commands. Take away from me reproach and contempt, for I observe your decrees. Though princes meet and talk against me, your servant

Psalms, Words of Praise and Wisdom

meditates on your statutes. Yes, your decrees are my delight; they are my counselors. I lie prostrate in the dust; give me life according to your word. I declare my ways, and you answered me; teach me your statues. Make me understand the way of your percepts, and I will mediate on your wondrous deeds. My soul weeps for sorrow; strengthen me according to your words. Remove from me the way of falsehood, and favor me with your law. The way of truth I have chosen; I have set your ordinances before me. I cling to your decrees; O LORD, let me not be put to shame. I will run the way of your commands when you give me a docile heart. Instruct me, O LORD; in the way of your statues, that I may exactly observe them. Give me discernment, that I may observe your law and keep it with all my heart. Lead me in the path of your commands, for in it I delight. Incline my heart to your decrees and not to gain. Turn away my eyes from seeing what is vain; by your way give me life. Fulfill for your servant your promise to those who fear you. Turn away from me the reproach which I dread, for your ordinances are good. Behold, I long for your percepts; in your justice give me life. Let your kindness come to me, O LORD, your salvation according to your promise. So shall I have an answer for those who reproach me, for I trust in your words. Take not the word of truth from my mouth, for in our ordinances is my hope. And I will keep your law continually, forever and ever. And I will walk at liberty, because I seek your precepts. I will speak of your decrees before kings without being ashamed. And I will delight in your commands, which I love. And I will lift up my hands to your commands and meditate on your statues. Remember your word to your servant since you have given me hope. My comfort in my affliction is that your promise gives me life. Though the proud scoff bitterly at me, I turn not away from your law. I remember your ordinances of old, O LORD, and I am comforted. Indignation seizes me because of the wicked who forsake your law. Your statues are the theme of my song in the place of my exile. By night I remember your name, O LORD, and I will keep your law. This has been mine, that I have observed your precepts. I have said, O LORD, that my part is to keep your words. I entreat you with all my heart. Have pity on me according to your promise. I considered my ways and turned my feet to your decrees. I was prompt and did not hesitate in keeping your commands. Though the snares of the wicked are twined about me, your law I have not forgotten. At midnight I rise to give you thanks because of your just ordinances. I am the companion of all who fear you and keep your precepts. Of your kindness, O LORD, the earth is full; teach me your statutes. You have done good to your servant, O LORD, according to your word. Teach me wisdom and knowledge, for in your commands I trust. Before I was afflicted I went astray, but now I hold to your promise. You are good and bountiful; teach me your statues. Though the proud forge lies against me, with all my heart I will observe your precepts.

Psalms, Words of Praise and Wisdom

Their heart has become gross and fat; as for me, your law is my delight. It is good for me that I have been afflicted, that I may learn your statutes. The law of your mouth is to me more precious than thousands of gold and silver pieces. Your hands have made me and fashioned me; give me discernment that I may learn your commands. Those who fear you shall see me and be glad, because I hope in your word. I know O LORD, that your ordinances are just, and in your faithfulness you have afflicted me. Let your kindness comfort me according to your promise to your servants. Let your compassion come to me that I may live, for your law is my delight. Let the proud be put to shame for oppressing me unjustly; I will meditate on your precepts. Let those turn to me who fear you and acknowledge your decrees. Let my heart be perfect in your statues, that I be not put to shame. My soul pines for your salvation; I hope in your word. My eyes strain after your promise; when will you comfort me? Though I am shriveled like a leathern flask in the smoke, I have not forgotten your statutes. How many are the days of your servant? When will you do judgment on my persecutors? The proud have dug pits for me; this is against your law. All your commands are steadfast; they persecute me wrongfully; help me! They have all but put an end to me on the earth, but I have not forsaken your precepts. In your kindness give me life, that I may keep the decrees of your mouth. Your word, O LORD, endures forever; it is firm as the heavens. Through all generations your truth endures; you have established the earth, and it stands firm. According to your ordinances they still stand firm; all things serve you. Had not your law been my delight, I should have perished in my affliction. Never will I forget your precepts, for through them you give me life. I am yours; save me, for I have sought your precepts. Sinners wait to destroy me, but I pay heed to your decrees. I see that all fulfillment has its limits; broad indeed is your command. How I love your law, O LORD! It is my meditation all the day. Your command has made me wiser than my enemies, for it is ever with me. I have more understanding than all my teachers when your decrees are my meditation. I have more discernment than the elders, because I observe your precepts. From every evil way I withhold my feet, that I may keep your words. From your ordinances I turn not away, for you have instructed me. How sweet to my palate are your promises, sweeter than honey to my mouth! Through your precepts I gain discernment; therefore I hate every false way. A lamp to my feet is your word, a light to my path. I resolve and swear to keep your must ordinances. I am very much afflicted; O LORD, give me life according to your word. Accept, O LORD, the free homage of my mouth, and teach me your decrees. Though constantly I take my life in my hands, yet I forget not your law. The wicked have laid a snare for me, but from your precepts I have not strayed. Your decrees are my inheritance forever; the joy of my heart they are. I intend in my heart to fulfill your statutes always, to the letter. I hate men of

Psalms, Words of Praise and Wisdom

divided heart, but I love you law. You are my refuge and my shield; in your word I hope. Depart from me, you wrongdoers, and I will observe the commands of my God. Sustain me as you have promised, that I may live; disappoint me not in my hope. Help me, that I may be safe and ever delight in your statutes. You despise all who stray from your statutes, for their deceitfulness is in vain. You account all the wicked of the earth as dross; therefore I love your decrees. My flesh shudders with dread of you, and I fear your ordinances. I have fulfilled just ordinances; leave me not to my oppressors. Be surety for the welfare of your servant; let not the proud oppress me. My eyes strain after your salvation and your just promise. Deal with your servant according to your kindness, and teach me your statues. I am your servant; give me discernment that I may know your decrees. It is time for the LORD to act: they have broken your law. For I love your command more than gold, however fine. For in all your precepts I go forward; every false way I hate. Wonderful are your decrees; therefore I observe them. The revelation of your words sheds light, giving understanding to the simple. I gasp with open mouth in my yearning for your commands. Turn to me in pity as you turn to those who love your name. Steady my footsteps according to your promise, and let no iniquity rule over me. Redeem me from the oppression of men, that I may keep your precepts. Let your countenance shine upon your servant, and teach me your statutes. My eyes shed streams of tears

Psalms, Words of Praise and Wisdom

because your law has not been kept. You are just, O LORD, and your ordinance is right. You have pronounced your decrees in justice and in perfect faithfulness. My zeal consumes me, because my foes forget your words. Your promise is very sure, and your servant loves it. I am mean and contemptible, but your precepts I have not forgotten.

Your justice is everlasting justice, and your law is permanent. Though distress and anguish have come upon me, your commands are my delight. Your decrees are forever just; give me discernment that I may live. I call out with all my heart; answer me, O LORD; I will observe your statues. I call upon you; save me, and I will keep your decrees. Before dawn I come and cry out; I hope in your words. My eyes greet the night watches in meditation on your promise. Hear my voice according to your kindness, O LORD; according to your ordinance give me life. I am attacked by malicious persecutors who are far from your law. You, O LORD, are near, and all your commands are permanent. Of old I know from your decrees, that you have established them forever. Behold my affliction, and rescue me, for I have not forgotten your law. Plead my cause, and redeem me; for the sake of your promise give me life. Far from sinners is salvation because they seek not your statutes. Your compassion is great, O LORD; according to your ordinances give me life. Though my persecutors and my foes are many, I turn not away from your decrees. I behold the apostates with

Psalms, Words of Praise and Wisdom

loathing, because they kept not to your promise. See how I love your precepts, O LORD; in your kindness give me life. Permanence is your word's chief trait; each of your just ordinances is everlasting. Princes persecute me without cause, but my heart stands in awe of your word. I rejoice at your promise, as one who has found rich spoil. Falsehood I hate and abhor; your law I love. Seven times a day I praise you for your just ordinances. Those who love your law have great peace, and for them there is no stumbling block. I wait for your salvation, O LORD, and your commands I fulfill. I keep your decrees and love them deeply. I keep your precepts and your decrees, for all my ways are before you. Let my cry come before you, O LORD; in keeping with your word, give me discernment. Let my supplication reach you; rescue me according to your promise. My lips pour forth your praise, because you teach me your statutes. May my tongue sing of your promise, for your commands are just. Let your hand be ready to help me, for I have chosen your precepts. I long for your salvation, O LORD, and your law is my delight. Let my soul live to praise you, and may your ordinances help me. I have gone astray [like a lost sheep]: seek your servant because your commands I do not forget.

Psalm 126(127):1-5
Unless the LORD build the house, they labor in vain who build it. Unless the LORD guard the city, in vain does the guard keep vigil. It is vain for you

Psalms, Words of Praise and Wisdom

to rise early, or put off your rest, you that eat hard-earned bread, for he gives to his beloved in sleep. Behold, sons are a gift from the LORD; the fruit of the womb is a reward. Like arrows in the hand of a warrior are the sons of one's youth. Happy the man whose quiver is filled with them; they shall not be put to shame when they contend with enemies at the gate.

Psalm 130(131)1-2
O LORD, my heart is not proud, nor are my eyes haughty; I busy not myself with great things, nor with things too sublime for me. Nay rather, I have stilled and quieted my soul like a weaned child.

Psalm 133(134):1-2
Come, bless the LORD, all you servants of the LORD who stand in the house of the LORD during the hours of night. Lift up your hands toward the sanctuary, and bless the LORD.

Psalm 137(138):1-6
I will give thanks to you, O LORD, with all my heart, [for you have heard the words of my mouth;] in the presence of the angels I will sing your praise; I will worship at your holy temple and give thanks to your name, because of your kindness and your truth; for you have made great above all things your name and your promise. When I called, you answered me; you built up strength within me. All the kings of the earth shall give thanks to you, O LORD, when they hear the words of your mouth;

Psalms, Words of Praise and Wisdom

and they shall sing of the ways of the LORD: "Great is the glory of the LORD." The LORD is exalted, yet the lowly he sees, and the proud he knows from afar. Though I walk amid distress, you preserve me; against the anger of my enemies you raise your hand; your right hand saves me. The LORD will complete what he has done for me; your kindness, O LORD, endures forever; forsake not the work of your hands.

Psalm 143(144):1-15
Blessed be the LORD, my rock, who trains my hands for battle, my fingers for war; my refuge and my fortress, my stronghold, my deliverer, my shield, in whom I trust, who subdues peoples under me. LORD, what is man, that you notice him; the son of man, that you take thought of him? Man is like a breath; his days, like a passing shadow. Incline your heavens, O LORD, and come down; touch the mountains, and they all smoke; flash forth lightning, and put them to flight, shoot your arrows, and rout them; reach out your hand from on high— deliver me and rescue me from many waters, from the hands of aliens, whose mouths swear false promises while their right hands are raised in perjury. O God, I will sing a new song to you; with a ten-stringed lyre I will chant your praise, you who give victory to kings, and deliver David, your servant. From the evil sword deliver me; and rescue me from the hands of aliens, whose mouth swear false promises while their right hands are raised in

perjury. May our sons be like plants well-nurtured in their youth, our daughters like wrought columns such as stand at the corners of the temple. May our garners be full, affording every kind of store; may our sheep be in the thousands, and increase to myriads in our meadows; may our oxen be well laden. May there be no breach in the walls, no exile, no outcry in our streets. Happy the people for whom things are thus; happy the people whose God is the LORD.

Psalm 145(146):1-10
Praise the LORD, O my soul; I will praise all my life; I will sing praise to my God while I live. Put not your trust in princes, in man, in whom there is no salvation. When his spirit departs he returns to his earth; on that day his plans perish. Happy he whose help is the God of Jacob, whose hope is in the LORD, his God, who made heaven and earth, the sea and all that is in them; who keeps faith forever, secures justice for the oppressed, gives food to the hungry. The LORD sets captives free; the LORD gives sight to the blind. The LORD raises up those that were bowed down; the LORD loves the just. The LORD protects strangers; the fatherless and the widow he sustains, but the way of the wicked he thwarts. The LORD shall reign forever; your God, O Sion, through all generations. Alleluia.

Psalms, Words of Praise and Wisdom

Psalm 148:1-13
Praise the LORD from the heavens, praise him in the heights; praise him, all you his angels, praise him, all you his hosts. Praise him sun and moon; praise him, all you shining stars. Praise him you highest heavens, and you waters above the heavens. Let them praise the name of the LORD, for he commanded and they were created; he established them forever and ever; he gave them a duty which shall not pass away. Praise the LORD from the earth, you sea monsters and all depths; fire and hail, snow and mist, storm winds that fulfill his word; you mountains and all you hills, you fruit trees and all you cedars; you wild beasts and all tame animals, you creeping things and you winged fowl. Let the kings of the earth and all peoples, the princes and all the judges of the earth, young men too, and maidens, old men and boys, praise the name of the LORD, for his name alone is exalted; his majesty is above earth and heaven, and he has lifted up the horn of his people. Be this his praise from all his faithful ones, from the children of Israel, the people close to him. Alleluia.

Psalms, Words of Praise and Wisdom

Psalm 150:1-6
Praise the LORD in his sanctuary, praise him in the firmament of his strength. Praise him for his mighty deeds, praise him for his sovereign majesty. Praise him with the blast of the trumpet, praise him with lyre and harp, praise him with timbrel and dance, praise him with strings and pipe. Praise him with sounding cymbals, praise him with clanging cymbals. Let everything that has breath praise the LORD! Alleluia.

Psalms, Words of Warning

Psalm 1:1-6
Happy the man who follows not the counsel of the wicked nor walks in the way of sinners, nor sits in the company of the insolent, but delights in the law of the LORD and meditates on his law day and night.
He is like a tree planted near running water, that yields its fruit in due season, and whose leaves never fade.[Whatever he does prospers.]
Not so the wicked, not so; they are like chaff which the wind drives away.
Therefore in judgment the wicked shall not stand, nor shall sinners, in the assembly of the just.
For the LORD watches over the way of the just, but the way of the wicked vanishes.

Psalm 4:3, 5
Men of rank, how long will you be dull of heart? Why do you love what is vain and seek after falsehood?
Tremble, and sin not; reflect, upon your beds, in silence.

Psalm 7:15-17
He who conceived iniquity and was pregnant with mischief, brings forth failure.
He has opened a hole, he has dug it deep, but he falls into the pit which he has made.
His mischief shall recoil upon his own head; upon the crown of his head his violence shall rebound.

Psalms, Words of Warning

Psalm 14:2-5
O LORD, who shall sojourn in your tent? Who shall dwell on your holy mountain?
He who walks blamelessly and does justice; who thinks the truth in his heart and slanders not with his tongue; who harms not his fellow man, nor takes up a reproach against his neighbor; by whom the reprobate is despised, while he honors those who fear the LORD; who though it be to his loss changes not his pledged word; who lends not his money at usury and accepts no bribe against the innocent.

Psalm 33(34):17
The LORD confronts the evildoers, to destroy remembrance of them from the earth.

Psalm 36(37):10, 12-18, 19-22, 32, 35, 36, 38
Yet a little while, and the wicked man shall be no more; though you mark his place he will not be there.
The wicked man plots against the just and gnashes his teeth at them; but the LORD laughs at him, for he sees that his day is coming.
A sword the wicked draw; they bend their bow to bring down the afflicted and the poor, to slaughter those whose path is right.
But their swords shall pierce their own hearts, and their bows shall be broken.
Better is the scanty store of the just than the great wealth of the wicked, for the power of the wicked shall be broken, but the LORD supports the just.

Psalms, Words of Warning

The LORD watches over the lives of the wholehearted; their inheritance lasts forever.

They are not put to shame in an evil time; in days of famine they have plenty.
But the wicked perish, and the enemies of the LORD, like the beauty of the meadows, vanish; like smoke they vanish.
The wicked man borrows and does not repay; the just man is kindly and gives, but those whom he blesses shall possess the land, while those he curses shall be cut off.
The wicked man spies on the just, and seeks to slay him.
I saw a wicked man, fierce, and stalwart as a flourishing, age-old tree.
Yet as I passed by, Lo! He was no more; I sought him, but he could not be found.
Sinners shall all alike be destroyed; the future of the wicked shall be cut off.

Psalm 49(50):16-23
But to the wicked man God says: "Why do you recite my statues, and profess my covenant with your mouth.
Though you hate discipline and cast my words behind you?
When you see a thief, you keep pace with him, and with adulterers you throw in your lot.
To your mouth you give free rein for evil, you harness your tongue to deceit.

Psalms, Words of Warning

You sit speaking against your brother; against your mother's son you spread rumors.

When you do these things, shall I be deaf to it? Or think you that I am like yourself? I will correct you by drawing them up before your eyes.
"Consider this, you who forget God, lest I rend you and there be no one to rescue you.
He that offers praise as a sacrifice glorifies me; and to him that goes the right way I will show the salvation of God."

Psalm 51(52):1-7, 8, 9
Why do you glory in evil, you champion of infamy? All the day you plot harm; your tongue is like a sharpened razor, you practiced deceiver!
You love evil rather than good, falsehood rather than honest speech.
You love all that means ruin, you of the deceitful tongue!
God himself shall demolish you; forever he shall break you; he shall pluck you from your tent, and uproot your from the land of the living.
The just shall look on with awe; then they shall laugh at him: "This is the man who made not God the source of his strength, but put his trust in his great wealth, and his strength in harmful plots."

Psalms, Words of Warning

Psalm 52(53):1-4
The fool says in his heart, "There is no God." Such are corrupt; they do abominable deeds; there is not one who does good.
God looks down from heaven upon the children of men to see if there be one who is wise and seeks God.
All alike have gone astray; they have become perverse; there is not one who does good, not even one.

Psalm 57(58):1-6
Do you indeed like gods pronounce justice and judge fairly, you men of rank? Nay, you willingly commit crimes; on earth you look to the fruits of extortion.
From the womb the wicked are perverted; astray from birth have the liars gone.
Theirs is poison like a serpent's, like that of a stubborn snake that stops its ears, that it may not hear the voice of enchanters casting cunning spells.

Psalm 58(59):13, 15-16
By the sin of their mouths and the word of their lips let them be caught in their arrogance, for the lies they have told under oath.
Each evening they return, they snarl like dogs and prowl about the city; they wander about as scavengers; if they are not filled, they howl.

Psalms, Words of Warning

Psalm 63(64):6-10
They resolve on their wicked plan; they conspire to set snares, saying, "Who will see us?"
They devise a wicked scheme, and conceal the scheme they have devised; deep are the thoughts of each heart.
But God shoots his arrows at them; suddenly they are struck.
He brings them down by their own tongues; all who see them nod their heads.

Psalm 81(82):2-4
"How long will you judge unjustly and favor the cause of the wicked? Defend the lowly and the fatherless; render justice to the afflicted and the destitute. Rescue the lowly and the poor; from the hand of the wicked deliver them."

Psalm 113B(115):2-8
"Why should the pagans say, "Where is their God?" Our God is in heaven; whatever he wills, he does. Their idols are silver and gold, the handiwork of men.
They have mouths but speak not; they have eyes but see not; they have ears but hear not; they have noses but smell not; they have hands but feel not; they have feet but walk not; they utter no sound from their throat.
Their makers shall be like them, everyone that trusts in them.

Psalms, Words of Warning

Psalm 134(135):15-18
The idols of the nations are silver and gold, the handiwork of men.
They have mouths but speak not; they have eyes but see not; they have ears but hear not, nor is there breath in their mouths.
Their makers shall be like them, everyone that trusts in them.

www.ingramcontent.com/pod-product-compliance
Lightning Source LLC
Chambersburg PA
CBHW040355190426
43201CB00037B/11